What a Waste
It Is To Lose One's Mind

The Unauthorized Autobiography
of Dan Quayle

Published by *The Quayle Quarterly*.

ISBN 0-9629162-2-6

10 9 8 7 6 5 4 3 2 1

The Quayle Quarterly is a political satire magazine,
"A Watchful Eye on the Vice Presidency."
Subscriptions are available for $14.95 (four issues per year).
Samples and back issues are available for $3.95 each, from:
The Quayle Quarterly, P.O. Box 8593, Brewster Station,
Bridgeport, CT, 06605.

The Quayle Quarterly invites reader comments, additions, or
corrections regarding this book. Please send correspondence to the
address above.

For spin-controlled information about the life of Vice President
Quayle, call (202) 456-2326.

My name is Danny Quayle,
I didn't go to Yale,
Got Cs and Ds at Indiana U.,
But what I profess is,
The key to my success is,
You talk like me
and you'll be famous, too...

> — From "Talk Like a Dan," to
> the tune of "Walk Like a
> Man," on the album *Georgie
> on my Mind* by The Capitol
> Steps.

Acknowledgements

We would like to thank Joe Fodor, who immersed himself in a sea of clippings and always came up with the one we were missing, and Michele Ruschhaupt, for her always excellent work. Jim and Mary Barry of Graphics Unlimited, we salute you for a job well done every single time.

Our thanks also go to writer and Quayle high school classmate Linda Marx for her many contributions and insights into the life of the young Dan.

We are grateful to the many Quayle watchers across the country who send us clippings and other bits of Quayle effluvia, especially our regular scouts Doc Taylor, Evelyn Shaw, Roger Roehl, Lorraine Anslow, Simon Nathan, and Robert Connelly.

We also would like to acknowledge, if not necessarily thank, the following:

George Herbert Walker Bush, for standing by his Dan, even in the face of the VP's overwhelming disapproval ratings from the American people;

Marilyn Quayle, for badgering Dan off of the golf course and into a life of public service;

And finally, Mr. Quayle, the *sine qua non* of this book. May history have nothing worse to say about him than that he made politics funny for a while. ■

"People that are really very weird can get into sensitive positions and have a tremendous impact on history."

— Dan Quayle, commenting on the book *Nicholas and Alexandra* by Robert K. Massey

Table of Contents

AP/Wide World Photo

"We cannot gamble with inexperience in that Oval Office."

— George Bush

Unauthorized Foreword

by George Herbert Walker Bush, President, United States of America

"Dan Quayle is a man of the future, a young man born in the middle of this century and from the middle of America. He's a dynamic young leader for the future of our party and the future of our nation."

"He has demonstrated his ability to get votes from women."

"He is a young man of vision, of character. One of Indiana's finest products, your man and mine..."

"I think he's getting a bum rap in the press."

"Take out the word 'Quayle' and insert the word 'Bush' wherever it appears, and that's the crap I took for eight years. Wimp. Sycophant. Lap dog. Poop. Lightweight. Boob. Squirrel. Asshole. George Bush."

"[Dan Quayle is] my choice, my first choice, and my only choice."

"He's different from me. I'm 64 and he's 41. And that's good, that's positive."

"I have great respect for him."

"He did not go to Canada, he did not burn his draft card and he damn sure didn't burn the American flag! And I am proud to have him at my side." ■

*"What a waste it is to lose
one's mind, or not to have a
mind is being very wasteful.
How true that is."*

— Dan Quayle, speaking at an
NAACP luncheon, 1989

Preface

"A Mind is a Terrible Thing to Waste."
— *The motto of the United Negro College Fund.*

During his first four years as vice president, Dan Quayle amused,
puzzled, and often frightened the country and the world with his
verbal misadventures. Consider Quayle's famous paraphrase of the
United Negro College Fund motto: "What a waste it is to lose one's
mind, or not to have a mind is being very wasteful. How true that
is." The updated edition of *Bartlett's Familiar Quotations* includes
these immortal words, thereby elevating our Vice President into the
company of such great speakers as Mark Twain, Will Rogers and
Yogi Berra.

We at *The Quayle Quarterly* have kept a watchful eye on Dan
Quayle for several years. Anticipating at least four more years with
Dan a mere heartbeat away from the leadership of the free world, we
felt it incumbent upon ourselves to further immortalize (or do we
mean immolate?) him.

This book is called an *auto*biography because it consists largely of
Quayle's own words. It is unauthorized, because the Quayle we've
chronicled is not the one he or his image-makers want us to see or
remember.

Besides, if this book really had been written by Dan Quayle, he
would have chosen a different title, like: "How to Succeed in Politics
Without Really Trying," or "Everything I Need to Know I'll Learn
Eventually."

Another good title might have been *Being There Too*, in honor of Jerzy Kozinski, who lived to see Dan Quayle become vice president, much like the unwitting Chauncey Gardiner in *Being There*. Kozinski predicted the rise of a simpleton with a blank slate of a background and telegenic good looks to a presidential candidacy, where he was to be a hapless and obedient puppet.

Certainly, we want this to be an entertaining book. Who would read a scholarly work on Dan Quayle? Yet we hope the point is clear, that when the emperor is wearing no clothes, the situation is at once humorous and grave.

Deborah Werksman
Jeff Yoder
Jefferson Morley

P.S. All the quotes herein in **boldface** type are verbatim from our Vice President. Read 'em and weep.

Timeline

1947   *Born February 4, Indianapolis, Indiana.*

My birth announcement:

*"He has been named James Danford [sic],
and will be another booster, or perhaps
assistant writer for Daddy's sports page."*

1965   *Graduated from Huntington High School.*

President of the Teen-Age Republicans.

*"I was not a very good student. I was very
average."*

1969   *Graduated from DePauw University, B.S., Political Science,
Grade Point Average: 2.16.*

*"Looking back, I should have pursued
philosophy and history and economics and
things of that sort in college more, but I
didn't."*

1969-1975   *Served in Indiana National Guard.*

*"The members of my generation who served
in Vietnam made a sacrifice for their
country that was far, far greater than mine."*

1970-1971   Chief investigator, consumer protection division of the Indiana Attorney General's office.

"It was just a job. It wasn't any special interest in consumer affairs. I needed a paycheck and the Attorney General said that I would be best to go down there, because he knew I was anti-consumer."

1972   Marries Marilyn Tucker. Three children: Tucker, born 1974, Benjamin, born 1977, and Corinne, born 1979.

"I don't know if she likes this, but in a way I treat her as a staff person."

1971-1973   Administrative assistant to Gov. Edgar D. Whitcomb.

1973-1974   Director, inheritance tax division of the Indiana Dept. of Revenue.

1974   Graduated from Indiana University School of Law, J.D., Grade Point Average: 2.74. Admitted to Indiana Bar.

"After all, let's ask ourselves: Does America really need 70 percent of the world's lawyers?"

1974-1976   *Associate publisher of his family newspaper,* Huntington
            Herald-Press.

            **"There was never anything where I've got to
            work really hard to get there."**

1976   *Elected to Congress, beating incumbent J. Edward Roush in
            Indiana's 4th Congressional District.*

            **The people have the freedom "to elect the
            representatives to represent them in a free
            representative democracy."**

1978   *Re-elected to second Congressional term.*

            **"I am not part of the problem. I happen to
            be a Republican."**

1980   *Elected to Senate, beating Birch E. Bayh.*

            **In the House "you can get a bunch of guys
            and go down to the gym and play basketball.
            You can't do that in the Senate."**

1986   *Re-elected to second Senate term.*

            **"I just don't believe in the basic concept that
            someone should make their whole career in
            public service."**

1988   *Selected by George Bush as his running mate.*

"George Bush has the experience, and with me the future."

1989   *Inaugurated as vice president of the United States.*

"I used to be a Batman fan until I had this job, now all of a sudden, Robin looks awfully good."

My grandfather Eugene C. Pulliam with his third wife, Nina, 1947.

"Family is something which goes back to the nucleus of civilization. And the very beginnings of civilization, the very beginnings of this country, goes back to the family."

— I said this two days before the 1988 election

Roots

My grandmother, Martha Ott Pulliam, was born March 23, 1891 in Franklin, Indiana. She was the daughter of Lyman Edward and Martha Payne Ott. I quoted my Nana, as we called her, during my debate with Lloyd Bentsen in 1988. She told me:

> *"You can do anything you want if you just set your mind to it and go to work."*

Martha graduated from Franklin College in Franklin, Indiana. In 1919 she married my grandfather, Eugene C. Pulliam, founder of Central Newspapers, Inc., a publisher of daily and weekly newspapers in Indiana and Arizona.

In 1941 Nana and Grandpa were divorced. Nana became publisher of *The Lebanon Reporter*. Grandpa became publisher of *The Indianapolis Star* and *News*, *The Arizona Republic* and *The Phoenix Gazette*. At his newspaper family/company picnics, he used to recite:

> *"Happy have we met;*
> *Happy have we been;*
> *Happy shall we be;*
> *Till we meet again."*

Later in life, Grandpa wrote front-page editorials about how John F. Kennedy was trying to "buy" the White House, and ordered that Robert F. Kennedy be given virtually no coverage in Indiana during his 1968 presidential campaign.

When Martin Luther King was shot and killed, Grandpa ordered the editor of *The Indianapolis Star* not to run his picture on the front page (the editor argued back and the photo ran.)

In 1943, Corrine Pulliam (their daughter and my Mom) married my father, James Quayle. My Dad's family business was Lincoln Logs, the little wooden building toys.

When I was chosen to run for vice president, my Dad said:

> *"It's like Reagan said about George [Bush],*
> *'I send him to all the funerals.'"*

My Mom (I love her) said:

> *"I'm going to disagree with you, I think he*
> *can do a lot for the country."*

Dad replied:

> *"Well, I hope he can, but he'd be the first*
> *[vice president] who ever did."*

I was born in Indianapolis on February 4, 1947. We lived in Huntington until I was eight years old.

I played Little League baseball for *The Huntington Herald-Press* team. When I was inducted into the Little League Hall of Excellence in 1991, the president of Little League baseball said:

> *"Little League baseball is a leadership
> training program and Vice President Quayle
> is an outstanding example of what can be
> achieved by adhering to the values learned
> while participating in Little League baseball."*

In 1955 my family moved to Phoenix, Arizona. It's really nice there:

> *"I love California. I grew up in Phoenix,
> Arizona. A lot of people forget that."*

Dad worked in public relations at *The Arizona Republic* and *The Phoenix Gazette*, and Mom supported conservative political candidates. We were a close family because:

> *"Republicans understand the importance of
> bondage between parent and child."*

We lived next to the eleventh tee at the Paradise Valley Country Club, and that's where I learned to play golf.

My mother said:

> *"Playing golf he learned how to control
> himself and to overcome his mistakes."*

I wrote a poem about my father in 1960, when I was 13 years old:

"My Dad is very very nice,
But he is not made of sugar and spice.
Sometimes he acts as if he has been disturbed
But at other times he is as cheerful as a bird."

Dad belonged to the John Birch Society, a secret anti-communist organization founded in 1958 by Massachusetts candymaker Robert Welch and named for a U.S. pilot shot down by Red Chinese during World War II.

Welch thought Dwight Eisenhower was a tool of international communism. Dad once compared Robert Welch to the prophet Nostradamus, and when he finally got to meet Welch, he said:

> *"[It] was like meeting the president of the*
> *United States."*

So you can understand why, around the Quayle house, civil rights and the environment weren't:

> *"things that we discussed a lot at the dinner*
> *table. The dinner table conversation was*
> *more along the lines of very strong*
> *anti-communist feelings. And then there*
> *were a lot of good discussions about what*
> *you would do on campus, or whether girls*
> *would be allowed to visit one's room —*
> *things of that sort. So it was a normal type*
> *of chit chat that sometimes got*
> *confrontational about what was socially*
> *acceptable and what wasn't.*

4

"...In our generation things were changing so fast and going on so quickly that I think all people of my generation had that little bit of rebellion and independence with your parents. But in my case never anything that was too extreme. There wasn't any social rebellion where I said, 'Parents, you really don't know what it's all about.' Because I was too close to my parents for that."

My DePauw University varsity golf team, 1969. That's me (team captain!) second from left.

> *"I was in college with the guy*
> *for three years and the only*
> *thing I remember is he was*
> *on the golf team and was*
> *quite a ladies' man."*

— Clark Adams, my former classmate

Ferris Bueller's Day Off

My family moved back to Huntington, Indiana in 1964; I attended
Huntington High and played on the golf team. I had a girlfriend
named Carla. A family friend said we:

> *"went to the drive-in movies a lot when he
> wasn't playing golf."*

I was the head of the Teen-Age Republicans, and I drove around
town with AuH2O license plates to support Barry Goldwater for
president (Au is the chemical symbol for "Gold" and H_2O is the
chemical symbol for "water.")

One of my high school classmates later said of me:

> *"He didn't know Goldwater's platform from
> Johnson's. He just wanted to attract attention
> to himself by advocating issues in front of
> everyone."*

But another high school girlfriend, Judy Feigel remembers:

> *"Dan was so determined to be someone, even
> then... He was very political."*

In September 1965 I enrolled at DePauw University:

> **"I didn't pay a lot of attention as I should
> have in college."**

My Dad described my college years:

> *"It was a great time. Dan drank booze and chased broads like his old man."*

I was on the golf team. My coach, Ted Katula, says I was aggressive but lazy.

I belonged to the same frat as George Bush: Delta Kappa Epsilon.

Some of my classmates derisively nicknamed me "Face Man."

Five of my former classmates from DePauw said that I had a reputation as a poor student who drank a lot and dated a lot of women. One of them, Joe Wirt, said I majored in "girls, golf and alcohol" at DePauw.

Clark Adams, another classmate, said:

> *"This is in 1968. To be politically apathetic in those years was to be a nonentity on campus. He was not a guy to take a position on anything except who his date was on Friday night and where to get drunk on Saturday night."*

I even failed my senior comprehensive exam in political science which I needed to graduate. But I later passed a substitute comprehensive exam.

I graduated with a 2.16 grade point average.

8

"I was a less than serious student in college. If I had to do it over again, I would be far more serious. I did play a lot of golf. But I don't think that's any reflection on my ability to lead this nation."

One of my fellow Goldwater campaign workers pouring "The Right Drink for the Conservative Taste."

UPI/Bettmann

120th Public Information Detachment of the Indiana National Guard, 1972. I'm second from the right in the back row. War is hell.

"We kept thinking next month
the war will be over and then
it would be another month.
No one figured four years
later we would still be
looking at Vietnam."

— Terry M. Skorcher, my frat bro'
and best friend at DePauw

All Quiet on the Midwestern Front

In April 1969 I received my draft notice.

> *"Like any 22-year-old college senior, when you are thinking about making a major decision in your life... and whether you are going to join the National Guard... you call home."*

Sure, some phone calls were made. I've admitted that. My parents and I "communicated" with Wendell C. Phillippi, a retired major general in the Guard and managing editor of the family newspaper.

> *"I hoped he would help me and I expected that."*

In May 1969, I was accepted into the Indiana National Guard. Robert Steele, one of my classmates from high school and from DePauw, was quoted as saying that he had been scheduled to be drafted in May 1969 and he tried to get into the Guard and couldn't. But I say:

> *"I got into the Guard fairly. There were no rules broken, to my knowledge."*

In December 1969 I was assigned to the 120th Public Information Detachment as a clerk/typist. Our job was to put out a magazine.

James Newland, Jr., who was in my unit and is now a reporter for the *The Indianapolis Star*, said:

> *"The magazine had a lot of mushy little*
> *feature stories in it that didn't require too*
> *much effort... We had some free time and it*
> *wasn't odd for us to drink some beer and*
> *play cards during an extended lunch break or*
> *after drill... we never failed to have a good*
> *time."*

Samuel R. Graves III, the supervisor of the 120th said:

> *"I wouldn't call us slackers. We did have*
> *some fun."*

James A. Gillaspy, another member of the unit, said:

> *"I do recall that on one occasion when he*
> *was there we had a hell of a good time.*
> *[Quayle] did his job like the rest of us. And*
> *when the job was done, he partied like the*
> *rest of us."*

I did not know in 1969 that I would be writing this book, I confess.
Back then:

Protesters demonstrate during my visit to Ohio, 1988.

"I, like many, many other Americans, had particular problems about the way the war was being fought. But, yes, I supported my president and I supported the goal of fighting Communism in Vietnam. My problem with the war was the no-win policy aspect... In a regional conflict, you have to have certain goals and the goal cannot be a no-win situation."

"I have a deep affection for those men and women who sacrificed their lives in Vietnam, and for anybody to imply anything differently is just simply wrong."

AP/Wide World Photo

"Who cares really? I've always told everybody I don't care if Danny smoked pot. I think it would make him a better person really."

— Brett Kimberlin, who claims to have sold marijuana to me during the 1970s

High Times

Brett Kimberlin, a convicted drug trafficker and bomber now serving time in a Federal penetentiary, claims that he met me at a frat party and subsequently sold marijuana to me 15 or 20 times during 1972:

> *"Well, I gave him a wedding present of some*
> *Afghanistan hashish and some Acapulco*
> *Gold. He was very appreciative."*

In 1977, as a first-term Congressman from Indiana, I told local reporter, Mark Helmke, that Congress should "definitely consider" decriminalizing possession of marijuana. I was troubled by the "disparity" of law enforcement efforts. Instead of expending time and effort to catch and prosecute marijuana users, I said:

> **"We should concentrate on prosecuting the**
> **rapists and burglars who are a menace to**
> **society."**

In 1982, a convicted drug dealer told the Drug Enforcement Administration that I had earlier bought cocaine and quaaludes for myself and South Carolina Senator Strom Thurmond in the men's room at the Indiana Press Club. At the time, the DEA was in the midst of a major inquiry into drug use on Capitol Hill. A special force running that investigation pursued the charge "properly and thoroughly," using "established investigative techniques," and found it to be false, the agency's statement said.

When asked in 1987 about Douglas Ginsberg, the Supreme Court nominee who had allegedly smoked marijuana, I said:

Doonesbury

BY GARRY TRUDEAU

> *"I don't believe [marijuana use] in and of itself would disqualify him. But particularly the fact that he admitted using it in the late 1960s and as recently as 1978 or 1979, that is a factor. It was not just a youthful indiscretion. Had it been a youthful indiscretion, it would have been less significant."*

In May 1988, George Bush said he was going to put his Veep in charge of the war on drugs. But he didn't give me that post after all.

In October 1988, Brett Kimberlin was thrown into solitary confinement on the orders of the Justice Department, which had been in contact with our campaign staff, to prevent him from holding a press conference at which he planned to talk about selling marijuana to me. Kimberlin is suing the Justice Department for violation of his civil rights.

In 1991, cartoonist Garry Trudeau found out about my DEA file and about Brett Kimberlin's lawsuit, and ran a series in "Doonesbury" about the "cover-up."

16

Doonesbury BY GARRY TRUDEAU

And boy, did Marilyn get mad! She said:

> *"I know the Vice President and I aren't going
> to tolerate it anymore. I haven't read
> 'Doonesbury' in five years. It hasn't been
> funny in five years."*

My family's paper, *The Indianapolis Star*, was the only newspaper in the country allowed to see my ultra-secret, confidential DEA file. *The Star* said the file exonerated me completely.

In August 1990, I urged the people of Peru to support the U.S. government's anti-narcotics program:

> *"It's a must... You are losing your children...
> just like we are losing our children."*

But while I object to Latin America's export of deadly drugs to this country, I think we should increase our export of deadly cigarettes to other countries.

I told tobacco people in North Carolina:

17

Doonesbury

BY GARRY TRUDEAU

"[While] the American public as a whole is smoking less... We have to think about the exports... [while] we're not going to back away from what public health officials say... we're not going to deny a country an export from our country because of that policy."

"Even though Federal health officials are promoting less tobacco use, the tobacco industry should continue to expand in foreign markets."

I deal with drugs as head of the Council on Competitiveness, reviewing FDA regulations on testing of new drugs. I have recommended shortening the FDA approval process. This is beneficial to Eli Lilly, a large Indianapolis pharmaceutical company to which my family, and George Bush, have many ties. George was a director on the board of Lilly, and they have been a generous contributor to my campaigns.

DANSBURY

BY G.B. TRUDEAU

THIS COMIC STRIP DRUG ALLEGATION IS LUDICROUS!!!

I'VE NEVER BOUGHT DRUGS IN MY LIFE! I'VE JUST SAID NO!!!

GB Trudeau

GO AHEAD AND CHECK MY DEA FILE... THERE'S NOTHING IN IT!!!

AND QUIT DRAWING ME AS A FEATHER!!!

THAT'S WHAT YOU'RE REALLY UPSET ABOUT, DAN...

OLIMAN THE OREGONIAN ©1991 BY TRIBUNE
WITH APOLOGIES TO TRUDEAU

The shingle for our law practice.

"Somehow he got in [to law school]; he talked his way in."

— James Quayle, my Dad

The Paper Chase

*"I was interested in joining the National
Guard because it enabled me to go to law
school as soon as possible."*

But I didn't go to law school right away. My grades at DePauw did
not meet the academic requirements of Indiana University's law
school. At Indiana U. Law in those days you needed a grade point
average of 2.6 to gain admission.

Because I got two Ds at DePauw and the rest of my grades were Cs
and a few Bs, my grade point average was a dismal 2.16. In fact, I
didn't even get a single A all through college (if I had, don't you
think I would have told David Broder and Bob Woodward when they
asked me, instead of "turning down the opportunity" to tell them how
many A's I got?).

I told them talking about my grades was:

"irrelevant and rather demeaning."

There were 1,200 applicants for 275 slots. I was admitted to law
school:

*"through an experimental Indiana University
program intended to offer 'equal
opportunity' to minorities, the economically
disadvantaged and other students of different
viewpoints and backgrounds."*

In short, I got into law school on affirmative action. Of course, my family had been an important donor to Indiana University for many years.

The dean of Indiana University Law School said:

> *"It's absolutely clear the program was not aimed at trying to benefit potentially influential or wealthy members of the Indiana community."*

I said:

> *"I got into law school fair and square. Nothing improper was done and no rules were broken."*

And besides:

> *"I deserve respect for the things I did not do."*

I graduated in 1974 with a 2.74 grade point average from law school — which was pretty good — about a B- average. Of course it didn't hurt my grades that I had married my brainy classmate, Marilyn Tucker.

"I think that, obviously, I would not have married Dan Quayle had I not thought that he was an equal to me."

— Marilyn Quayle

She Stoops to Conquer

Ode to the Flipster

> *"She grew up in the 50s,*
> *loving Lucy, liking Ike*
> *When good boys rode a T-bird,*
> *and bad ones rode a bike.*
> *Elvis and his pelvis may have seemed*
> *so very hip,*
> *But not to Marilyn Tucker,*
> *the Hoosier with a flip."*

I met Marilyn Tucker at a law school gathering and we were married 10 weeks later by the law school dean. She says she was attracted to my "intellectual curiosity."

Our first child's due date coincided with Marilyn's bar exam so she had labor induced 10 days early.

In 1974 we moved to Huntington and opened our law firm, Quayle & Quayle. Marilyn ran the practice while I worked as associate publisher at my family's paper. Two years later the Allen County Republican chairman asked me if I wanted to run for Congress against the popular Democrat Ed Roush.

Marilyn said:

> *"We thought it was a joke when he asked Dan*
> *to run."*

Marilyn acted as my campaign manager, and we beat Roush in 1976

Then, as Marilyn said:

> "... we decided the best role I could play for
> him ... would [be to] continue my role as an
> adviser to him. And every briefing he had I
> would sit in on, all the position papers that
> were written I would go through, I would
> critique his speeches and he would use me as
> his adviser, the final person he went to before
> he made his decision. "

Bob Rowe, who used to head my regional office in Fort Wayne,
Indiana, said:

> "About the only thing Marilyn wouldn't
> express an opinion on is how to hold a golf
> club."

In fact, in 1991, when CBS taped my guest appearance on "Major
Dad," in which I played myself, Marilyn made sure the camera crew
put the children's photos next to hers on my desk, and read and
edited the script herself.

We had a rough time during the 1988 campaign. Marilyn told the
National Press Club:

> "It hurt reading stories or seeing reports
> about a man bearing almost no resemblance
> to the one I love deeply. At times I felt

*misunderstood, misrepresented, very angry
and terribly vulnerable."*

Marilyn was criticized for her flip. The January 1990 issue of
Mirabella designated her hairstyle:

> *"the worst of the millenium; worse than the
> pompadour, the bouffant and the beehive."*

AP/Wide World Photo

And, she was on Blackwell's 1990 ten worst-dressed list, for her
"1940s librarian" look. But the February 1991 issue of *Vogue* called
her "The New Marilyn."

Being the wife of the vice president took some adjustment for
Marilyn. At first she felt that the position lacked spontaneity.
Marilyn has a "prankish" sense of humor. Once during the '88
campaign she got me to sit on a whoopee cushion.

MARILYN QUAYLE

Marilyn Quayle

Inauguration Day
January 20, 1989

Commemorative envelope from the 1990 Inauguration.

According to Marilyn:

> *"I'm having fun. Far more fun than I thought
> I'd have."*

Marilyn has taken on two official causes: disaster preparedness and
breast cancer prevention. In Bangladesh, she unloaded relief
supplies for three minutes and and spent about five distributing rice,
clothes and candles. Of course security preparations for her visit
diverted helicopter time and manpower, but it was a great photo op.

To prevent breast cancer, Marilyn thinks both boys and girls should
be educated, since it is often a boyfriend or husband who first notices
the symptoms.

My staff is a little apprehensive that this outspokenness might offend my right-wing supporters.

But they'll be okay when they read her new novel, co-authored with her sister, Nancy Northcott. Entitled *Embrace the Serpent*, it is about what happens when Cuban leader Fidel Castro suddenly drops dead and the Russians secretly hand-pick his successor. *Publishers Weekly* praised the novel's "Democrat-bashing, tin-ear dialogue and soapbox style narration... painful prose and political point-making." Marilyn and her sister are writing another one which I bet will be just as good.

Marilyn likes to call herself a "professional woman" and at one point considered becoming a commentator on "USA Today on TV" opposite former California Governor Jerry Brown. I nixed that idea.

Sometimes my staff only learns what Marilyn is up to by reading about it in the paper.

Marilyn sums up her life this way:

> *"When I look at my life, it's moved so quickly! I wasn't going to get married — and then I got married so quickly. I wasn't going to have children — I did. Dan wasn't going to go into politics — now he's the vice president. I don't plan."*

I sum it up like this:

> **"Dick [Cheney] and I have something in common. That is that we both overmarried."**

Paula Parkinson, lobbyist and Playboy model.

"Anybody who knows Dan
Quayle knows he would
rather play golf than have
sex any day."

— Marilyn Quayle

Everything You Always Wanted to Know About Sex

In January 1980 Representatives Thomas B. Evans Jr. (R-DE), Tom Railsback (R-IL), and I went golfing in posh Atlantis, Fla., where we shared a cottage with Paula Parkinson, a lobbyist who later posed nude for *Playboy*. This incident sparked a Congressional investigation into the so-called "sex for votes" scandal.

Parkinson said I propositioned her while we danced at a restaurant in Palm Beach, but she turned me down.

During 1988, the sex for votes issue came up again, and Marilyn sent me out of the house to face the press with a bagful of garbage as a symbol of what we thought about the allegations.

Sex came up again, in 1990, when I was visiting Chile for the inauguration of President Patricio Aylwin. I bought this anatomically correct wooden doll for $4.00. I said:

> *"I could take this home, Marilyn. This is something teen-age boys might find of interest."*

Later, I told the press I had shown the doll to Margaret Thatcher.

Then, in 1991, when I heard that basketball star Magic Johnson had tested positive for the AIDS virus, and was going to become the spokesman for "safe sex," I took that as an opportunity to talk about my own sexual preferences:

"If there is something I can do, it is not to encourage young people to practice safe sex, but to emphasize abstinence. That's a sure cure.
"If you look at people's values in certain areas, there are risks. I will talk out on the importance of family and family values. There is a lot of risk out there, but abstinence is one way to prevent this."

Cargill Photo, Monroe, CT

Anatomically correct doll like the one I bought in Chile.

The anatomically correct Dan Quayle doll is made by the same Chilean artisans who created the doll that I bought.

Here I am, with Pat Robertson and Jesse Helms, where church and state meet.

> *"My friends, we can and we will, never, never surrender to what is right."*

— This is what I told Pat
   Robertson's Christian Coalition

Heaven Can Wait

*"Religion is everything to me. We try to
practice what God has communicated to us...
Religion is life and life after life."*

Marilyn grew up a practicing Presbyterian, but her father thought the
Presbyterians were too soft on homosexuality, so he left the church
and found a new spiritual leader in Houston evangelist Col. Robert
Thieme. A real-life Air Force Colonel who wears his uniform when
he delivers his sermons, Thieme is pretty conservative. His sermons
come on cassette tapes you send away for, with titles like "Scar
Tissue of the Soul," "Satanic Plot #1," and "Slave Market of Sin."

Marilyn once admitted:

*"I read Dr. Thieme's literature and I do find
him very good and enjoy listening to his
tapes."*

But I disclaimed:

*"She doesn't listen to them now. I don't
believe I've listened to any Thieme tapes...
Well — my wife listens to the tapes once in a
while. It's her family that's involved with
him."*

I told Richard Fenno that I don't relate to the right wing of the party. But I'm not against mixing up religion and politics; I once told a group of teachers:

"Let me just say as one Christian to another, it's time for the Christians of this country to come out of the closet and come to the polling booth and make the country work again."

National prayer service at Washington Cathedral, January 1989.

*"I wanted to be a golf pro,
but my family pushed me into
politics."*

— I said this once to a family friend.

Caddyshack

My golf bag once saved my life. I hid under it at a low spot on a Chicago golf course 20 years ago as a tornado demolished a nearby shed.

While I play golf around the country today, Secret Service agents carry around the "football," the black case that holds the codes necessary for me to order a nuclear attack.

My Secret Service agents know me well — they've given me the code name "Scorecard."

My handicap is a 7.

In May 1991, while John Sununu was under attack for personal use of military airplanes, I took a golf trip to Augusta, Ga. with then-Secretary of Transportation Samuel Skinner. We flew on a 12-seat military plane with a five member Air Force crew. Estimated cost to the taxpayers: $27,000.

Shortly after the 1988 election, I played 18 holes at the restricted Seminole Golf Club in Palm Beach. Jews and blacks aren't allowed, and the media was outraged.

Then, in 1990, after one round at Monterey's all-white, all-male Cypress Point Golf Course, former home of the Bing Crosby tournaments, I had to cancel the rest of my games because of public pressure.

But I've kept my honorary membership at the all-male Burning Tree Country Club outside of Washington:

> *"I've played there before and I'll play there again. I'm not going to protest Burning Tree. Maybe they'll change. I think it would be a good idea for them to take women into the club. I don't have any problem playing there in the meantime."*

My staff knows to schedule important meetings several hours before I leave for the golf course. One aide said:

> *"He goes on a high."*

I get distracted by my eagerness to get to the course, so events can't be scheduled too close to tee time.

> *"I can't get enough of it!"*

Here I am with Bryant Gumbel. Who says I only play at clubs that exclude black people?

41

Robert Redford in The Candidate.

"I'll have to check with my Dad."

— What I said upon being asked to
run for Congress

"Go ahead; you won't win."

— James C. Quayle, my Dad

The Candidate

In 1972, my friend Frank Pope and I went to see the movie "The Candidate." It inspired me. Frank said we:

> *"ended up talking all night about the movie*
> *— and politics. Danny's dream was to have*
> *a political career that could ultimately*
> *culminate in his being governor of Indiana."*

I said:

> *"In college...I was never involved in student*
> *government. I didn't run for student body*
> *president. But when I worked in the*
> *governor's office, I looked around and*
> *thought, 'This is fun.' That's when I first*
> *thought about going into politics. I thought*
> *about moving back to Huntington and*
> *running for state representative. I had my*
> *eye on an incumbent Democrat who had*
> *been in office for a while. But I never*
> *thought about running for Congress."*

In March 1976, the Allen County Republican chairman asked me to be the Republican candidate for Congress:

> *"I told him that I wouldn't even consider it*
> *unless they guaranteed me that I'd have no*
> *primary opposition and unless they would*
> *raise money for me."*

My campaign literature pointed out my resemblance to Robert Redford, until the liberal actor sent me a telegram asking me to stop.

After I won with 55 percent of the vote, I sent Redford an autographed picture of myself.

In the 1980 Senate campaign I again compared myself to Redford, and Redford sent another telegram to me asking me to "cease and desist." I won that election with 53.8.% of the vote. By the 1988 presidential campaign Redford had given up trying to stop me from comparing myself to him and began greeting people with

> *"Hello everybody, I'm Dan Quayle."*

During my campaign against Democratic incumbent Ed Roush, one of my precinct workers was going to drive an elderly voter to the polls, until the woman said she wasn't going to vote for me. The precinct worker dumped her right back in her driveway and said:

> *"Well, if that's the way you feel about it, let*
> *Ed Roush drive you to the polls."*

Marilyn tells that story with relish, adding:

> *"That is what it takes to win!"*

And I agree with her:

*"I beat incumbents. And believe me, you
don't beat incumbents by saying we're all
going to do a good job and I'm a nice guy.
You beat incumbents by going for the
jugular and by hammering at the issues over
and over again."*

Of course, it helps if your opponent underestimates you. The next
incumbent I beat, Senator Birch Bayh said:

*"C'mon boys, don't bother me. I'm debating
Danny Quayle. The boy's retarded."*

It may be superstitious of me to go to the dentist every election day,
but it's brought me good luck so far.

Once I got to Washington, I had this to say:

*"To be quite blunt about it I'm not
impressed with the overall caliber of
members of the House."*

Indeed, I described my House career as follows:

*"My first year [1977] I spent getting my
family moved to Washington. The second
year I ran for re-election. Then as soon as I
was elected, I started running for the
Senate."*

While a Senator, I said:

> *"I feel that this [1981] is my first year, that next year is an election year, that the third year is the mid point and that the fourth year is the last chance I'll have to make a record since the last two years, I'll be a candidate again. Everything I do in those last two years will be posturing for the election. But right now I don't have to do that."*

Once I became VP, I had this to say about Congress:

> *"The only thing Congress is interested in... is getting re-elected. I'll never forget the first time I came to this town in 1976, the first item on the agenda and the only item on the agenda was just to get re-elected. Forget the policy, forget the substance. Just get re-elected. I was appalled in 1976 and I'm appalled now."*

In 1978, when I was running for re-election to the House of Representatives, George Bush, who was himself gearing up for his 1980 presidential bid, made campaign appearances for me.

Preparing for the campaign, I put this question to my staff:

> *"What are we going to say about me before I got into politics — that I was a newspaperman?"*

> *"No, we'll call you Dan Quayle, student. How about Dan Quayle, father?*

*After all, you were only twenty-nine; we'll
just say you never did anything else."*

**"If I had not run for the Senate, I would
have run for one more term and then I
would have looked around for something
else. I might have gotten out of politics. But
I didn't want to stay in the House. Ever
since I was elected, I thought about the
Senate if anything came up. So you could
say I had my eyes set on the Senate for a
long time."**

One of my top campaign workers said:

*"People called him 'wet head' because he
was always coming out of the [House] gym.
His attendance record was lousy... They
didn't know where he was a lot of the time.
He'd be in the gym or he'd sneak off to play
golf and they'd have to call all around to find
him."*

A Washington staffer said:

*"He would miss meetings, miss votes. He'd
meet [Rep. Tom] Railsback who would say,
'Let's play golf,' and off they'd go."*

I missed 10 of 14 Small Business Committee meetings during one
period of time, and 40 of 61 meetings of the Foreign Affairs
Committee during another.

Here I am with my buddy, Teddy.

In 1987 I was criticized by veterans' groups for missing a vote on funding for homeless vets because I was playing in a golf tournament.

I was careful not to get onto a controversial committee:

> *"I know one committee I don't want —*
> *Judiciary. They are going to be dealing with*
> *all those issues like abortion, bussing, voting*
> *rights, prayers. I'm not interested in those*
> *issues and I want to stay as far away from*
> *them as I can."*

Some of my House colleagues described me as being:

"about a quarter of an inch deep."

I don't know why they said that. I supported some very meaningful legislation.

For example, in 1978 I introduced a bill that would have cut off food stamps for striking coal miners and their families.

In 1980 I proposed giving a 50 percent income tax credit, up to $150, for people who lose weight or stop smoking.

In 1986, I added a provision to the tax reform bill that would allow foreign golfers to stay in the country and remain tax exempt for a longer period of time.

Other than that, my only major piece of legislation was co-sponsored by Teddy Kennedy. The Job Training Partnership Act replaced the Comprehensive Employment and Training Act.

"People come up to me and talk about it. They compare it to CETA. It's doing especially well in Indiana. We found out the other day that 73,000 trainees have gotten jobs. The key is the domination of the Private Industry Councils (PICs) by business."

*"We held hearings on it around the state
this year. It gave people a chance to come in
and praise the program. Most of them have
— especially the business community. They
are strongly behind it... The program is
criticized for what is called 'creaming' —
that we are training the unemployed, but the
easiest of the unemployed, that we don't
reach down to help the hard-core
unemployed. I'm not sure whether that is
the case or not."*

One critic called the JTPA:

"an awful mess."

Another called it corporate welfare, saying that putting the PICs in
charge is like setting up:

*"a welfare system that left it up to welfare
mothers to determine how much money they
should get."*

In September 1985 *Politics in America* judged me one of "the twelve
most effective but underrated" members of Congress for being an:

*"unpretentious, rarely partisan legislative
professional... candid, well informed and not
prone to self-promotion."*

"All the reporters ask me about my failures.
Are they kidding? There are no failures.
Failure? Failure isn't in my vocabulary."

"I haven't had many failures. So I just keep
going on the theory that when you're hot
you're hot. Now what will happen when the
roof caves in on me, I don't know. It hasn't
yet. And I never think of it doing so ... I've
risen very fast — first office, Congress; two
terms; then the Senate. I never earned my
spurs, as they say. And I guess I'm still
flying high."

Now that I'm in the executive branch with a Democratic Congress, I
say:

I support "efforts to limit the terms of
members of Congress, especially members of
the House and members of the Senate."

UPI/Bettmann

"I stand by all the misstatements that I've made."

— I said this in 1988, and I still mean it

Fear and Loathing on the Campaign Trail '88

"One word sums up probably the responsibility of any vice president, and that one word is 'to be prepared.'"

"I'm going to be a vice president very much like George Bush was. He proved to be a very effective vice president, perhaps the most effective we've had in a couple of hundred years."

When George called me at the convention and told me I was going to be his running mate, I jumped in the shower, put on fresh clothes, and thought:

"Well, now, what am I going to say?"

I arrived at the Spanish Plaza in New Orleans and when George introduced me to the crowd it was like I couldn't stop grapping him around the shoulders, flapping my arms and shouting:

"Let's go get 'em. All right? You got it?"

I was assigned to work with my handlers, Stu Spencer and Joe Canzeri, but I rebelled and winged it at an appearance in Chicago, with predictably disastrous results:

"Why did you let him?"

asked Canzeri. Spencer replied:

> *"I want[ed] him to step on his dick, and then we'll own him again."*

The debate between me and Democratic vice presidential nominee, Senator Lloyd Bentsen, was my biggest test of the election. I had practiced for weeks with my handlers. Judy Woodruff of *The MacNeil-Lehrer Newshour* asked the first question:

> *"Why do you think that you have not made a more substantial impression on some of the people who have been able to observe you up close?"*

I answered:

> *"The question goes to whether I am qualified to be vice president, and in the case of tragedy, whether I'm qualified to be president. Qualifications for the office of vice president or president are not age alone. We must look at the accomplishments and we must look at the experience. I have more experience than others who have sought the office of vice president.*

*Now let's look at the qualifications and let's
look at the three biggest issues that are going
to be confronting America in the next
presidency. These issues are national
security and arms control, jobs and
education, and the Federal budget deficit.
On each one of those issues I have more
experience than does the Governor of
Massachusetts."*

So far, so good, right? But then they asked me the same question
three more times. I answered:

*"It's not age, it's accomplishments, it's
experience. I have far more experience than
many others who have sought the office of
vice president of this country. I have as
much experience in the Congress as Jack
Kennedy did when he sought the
presidency."*

Lloyd Bentsen went in for the kill:

*"Senator, I served with Jack Kennedy. I
knew Jack Kennedy. Jack Kennedy was a
friend of mine. Senator, you're no Jack
Kennedy."*

I cried out:

"That was really uncalled for, Senator."

Bentsen turned to me and said:

> "You're the one that was making the
> comparison, Senator, and I'm the one who
> knew him well. And frankly, I think you're so
> far apart in the objectives that you choose for
> your country that I did not think the
> comparison was well taken. Senator."

We won the election anyway, but it was no fun, especially for
Marilyn. She said:

> "1988 was a baptism of fire for the Quayles.
> Before it was over I felt at least a little
> singed."

I agree:

> "Was my confidence shaken? I don't know
> anybody who would go through that kind of
> an ordeal — you'd have to be a little bit
> shaken. It was so intense."

In 1988 we were shaked and baked.

TWISTED IMAGE by Ace Backwords ©1990

Here I am with a Salvadoran death squad leader, pointing a flame thrower at my elbow.

"I believe we are on an irreversible trend toward more freedom and democracy — but that could change."

— I said this about the New World Order, before there even was one

It's a Mad, Mad, Mad, Mad World

One of the best parts of my job as vice president is all the travel, like going to state funerals:

> *"There is a ceremony for the funerals, but you can also do a lot of work. You can meet a lot of people..."*

In the Spring of 1989, I visited American Samoa, where I told the people who came to meet me at the airport:

> *"You all look like happy campers to me. Happy campers you are, happy campers you have been, and as far as I'm concerned, happy campers you will always be."*

In June 1989, I went to El Salvador. I warned El Salvador's most prominent right-wing politician, Roberto d'Aubuisson, to respect human rights. I said that the United States would:

> *"work towards the elimination of human rights in El Salvador."*

When Czechoslovakia broke free of communism, I marvelled:

"Who would have predicted that Dubcek,
who brought the tanks in in Czechoslovakia
in 1968 is now being proclaimed a hero in
Czechoslovakia?"

I guess I had my history a little mixed up. Turns out Dubcek is a
hero because he resisted the Russians, who dragged him away in
handcuffs.

In January 1990, I got a chance to work the Panama Canal locks
during a visit to Panama City:

"I felt like I was in charge."

On my way to Venezuela I phoned Richard Nixon for advice —
when he was there in 1958 they stoned his car. But I had better luck:

"And let me tell you, the people that I met,
whether it was in Honduras or Jamaica,
obviously, Panama, just people on the street,
not one time did I get a negative response
about the United States. As a matter of fact,
I didn't even get a, you know, a real thumbs
down or the raspberries as you drove by, a
better reception, quite frankly, in a couple of
cities there than you might even get in —
here at home."

In March 1990, while visiting Santiago, Chile, I told Latin American
leaders how to handle a photo opportunity:

"You smile discreetly. Look like you're enjoying yourself, like you're ready to get down to serious business. You've got to be careful what you say."

Everywhere I go, I manage to get in a little fun. In Singapore I was late for a meeting with the Prime Minister because I was playing golf, and I kept the Indonesian Vice President waiting for two hours while Marilyn and I went scuba diving.

Richard Nixon told me I should leave my golf clubs at home when I travel, but I say:

"It's just the political instincts I have. I don't want to be whisked into embassies. The better I do personally, the better the country does."

My political instincts on display in Sydney, Australia, 1989.

"The [Competitiveness] Council is acting as a nefarious, secret kind of government, outside the constitutional and democratic processes for enacting laws."

— Rep. Henry Waxman (D-CA)

How to Succeed in Business

I am the head of the Council on Competitiveness, which is staffed from my office. We review Federal agency regulations and make changes to them.

> *"The president gave me this task because he sensed that many regulations he got off the books are coming back on."*

Unlike other executive committees, we do not allow public scrutiny of the records of our meetings or our phone conversations with business groups.

We are working to:

■ Remove protection from millions of acres of wetlands. When asked about how to define wetlands, I said:

> *"How about if we say when it's wet, it's wet?"*

■ Weaken Clean Air Act regulations:

> *"Our future competitiveness demands that true environmentalists and responsible leaders not allow the well-intentioned concerns of the American public to be manipulated and exploited as a means to re-establish unnecessary regulatory, economic and social controls."*

■ Make it harder for victims of unsafe products to recover damages:

> *"Somehow there's this idea that if someone has deep pockets, just let them pay and it's going to be a freebie... The product liability laws in this country are ridiculous. There's no sense of certainty, there are no limitations... If you look at comparative disadvantages with other countries, product liability must rank right up there as one of the premier candidates."*

We are also working to:

■ Weaken nutrition labelling regulations;
■ Weaken airplane noise reduction standards;
■ Delay tough new quality standards for medical laboratories;
■ Oppose legislation that would tighten auto fuel economy standards;
■ Fight a ban on burning of lead acid batteries;
■ Gut a recycling requirement for incinerators.

In December 1991, the director of the Competitiveness Council, Allan Hubbard, was charged with conflict of interest because he reviews regulations that help companies in which he owns stock. But, in June 1991, I had given him a highly unusual blanket waiver of conflict of interest laws.

Meanwhile, citizens' groups are suing the Council for withholding information. We claim to be operating under "executive privilege."

We are, in the words of Rep. Waxman:

*"beyond public accountability and beyond
the law of the land."*

But I'm no dummy. Big business makes big campaign contributions:

**"I do have a political agenda. It's to have as
few regulations as possible."**

UPI/Bettmann

*"Mars is essentially in the
same orbit... somewhat the
same distance from the sun,
which is very important. We
have seen pictures where
there are canals, we believe,
and water. If there is water,
that means there is oxygen.
If oxygen, that means we can
breathe."*

— I really did say this

The Last Frontier

As head of the National Space Council, I coordinate space policy between NASA and other government agencies:

> *"People have asked the question, can NASA do the job? My answer is simply, you bet NASA can do the job."*

I wholeheartedly support the new Freedom Space Station, and I was very enthusiastic when I was briefed by NASA:

> *"As a matter of fact, I didn't understand it all. Only thing I know is that it looked good."*

U.S. scientists have criticized the space station, but I say:

Tom Clancy in battle gear

> *"The importance of the space station is not in the power of its circuits, it is in the size of the dream."*

I once said SDI would work because it saved the day in Tom Clancy's novel *Red Storm Rising*:

> *"They're not just novels, they're read as the real thing."*

I then asked Clancy to act as a consultant to the National Space Council. I believe that:

>*"Our space program should always go full throttle up. Let me be clear: That is not just our ambition. That is our destiny."*

Why? I'll tell you why:

>*"We are leaders of the world of the space program. We have been the leaders of the world of our... of the space program and we're going to continue where we're going to go, notwithstanding the Soviet Union's demise and collapse — the former Soviet Union — we now have independent republics which used to be called the Soviet Union. Space is the next frontier to be explored. And we're going to explore. Think of all the things we rely upon in space today: Communications from... Japan, detection of potential ballistic missile attacks. Ballistic missiles are still here. Other nations do have ballistic missiles. How do you think we were able to detect some of the Scud missiles and things like that? Space, reconnaissance, weather, communications — you name it. We use space a lot today."*

Blackboard Jungle

I was awarded the IgNobel Prize for Education by MIT for being:

"a consumer of time and occupier of space, and for demonstrating, better than anyone else, the need for science education."

This is what I have to say about education:

"Quite frankly, teachers are the only profession that teach our children. It's a unique profession and, by golly, I hope when they go into the teaching field that they do have that zeal and they do have that mission and they do believe in teaching our kids and they're not getting into this just as a job or a way to put food on the table."

"We will move forward. We will move upward and, yes, we will move onward."

"We're going to have the best educated American people in the world."

Here I am with the fightin' Kuwaiti Air Force,
New Year's Day, 1991.

"We are ready for any
unforeseen event that may or
may not occur."

— I said this about U.S.
  preparedness for the Gulf War

The Red Badge of Courage

"The world is still a dangerous place."

When the Gulf War started, I met with the president every day. You could see my picture in the White House photos.

David Beckwith, my press secretary, said:

> *"He's been in every meeting from the
> beginning. He's been in virtually every
> meeting the President's been in and a couple
> that he hasn't been in. He doesn't discuss
> the advice he gives, but he's there and he
> participates."*

Craig Whitney, my assistant deputy press secretary, explained:

> *"Before he left for vacation, when everything
> was heating up, he was involved in all the
> early decisions."*

This war was different from the other one that I vociferously supported but declined to actually fight in:

> *"Vietnam is a jungle... Kuwait, Iraq, Saudi
> Arabia, you have sand."*

And, of course:

"Operation Desert Storm is truly a just war,
a battle of good against evil."

I paid a visit to the troops stationed in the Gulf over the New Year.
Boy, were they happy to see me. Nobody booed at me, or anything.

While I was there, I inadvertently blurted out the precise location of
the U.S. Air Force's Stealth bomber base in Saudi Arabia on a live
TV interview. I also said:

> *"I'll tell you one person who doesn't think*
> *we've wasted our money on $600 toilet seats*
> *— Saddam Hussein."*

In fact, when I was on the Senate Armed Services Committee, I
defended the inefficient and corrupt Pentagon procurement system:

> *"In the past we have tried too much to*
> *prevent the making of mistakes."*

If I was in charge, we just might use nuclear weapons:

> *"[It is] always an option, an option you are*
> *not going to rule out."*

Of course, if the United States is still a representative democracy
when I'm president, I'll have to deal with that annoying Congress. I
told the Republican Governors' Association's Annual Conference
that:

> *"By portraying themselves as the party of peace, and the Administration as the party of war, some Congressional Democrats... seem to have placed partisanship above statesmanship."*

Waging war is tough! Especially in a country with freedom of the press and the right to free assembly:

> *"There have been some [anti-war] demonstrations... unfortunately, the media seem compelled to devote much more attention to those protests than they deserve."*

Still, we won (didn't we?). As I told a gathering of the American Society of Newspaper Editors, the Persian Gulf war was:

> *"a stirring victory for the forces of aggression against lawlessness."*

"If we don't succeed, we run the risk of failure."

— I said this about efforts to get a Republican majority in Congress

Other People's Money

"I am now cashing in on being vice president for others. They'll remember me. I'll remember them."

I raised about $16 million for the Republican party during 1989 and 1990, appearing at about 120 fundraisers.

People paid $100 each to eat hors d'oeuvres and hear me speak in Austin, Tx. Others forked over $1,000 each to have their photograph taken with me. $2,500 contributors got to sit on stage while I spoke. I appeared at a $1,000-a-plate breakfast fund-raiser in Savannah, Ga. for Republican gubernatorial nominee Johnny Isakson. In New York, you could have dined with me at the Plaza for $5,000, or paid $1,000 to attend a reception.

There was a scheme afoot in New York to charge $20,000 to play a round of golf with me, but it got a lot of bad publicity.

I said of the Republican party:

"One thing we're able to do is raise money."

Marilyn, my wife and political adviser, points out:

"If you're an incumbent you can win because everything's stacked in your favor. Money wins."

"You don't make money in politics. Or, I should say—you shouldn't."

— Marilyn Quayle

The Ruling Classes

My 1988 adjusted gross income: $156,546

My 1989 adjusted gross income: $133,696

My 1990 adjusted gross income: $121,126

Our supporters contributed $340,000 (tax-deductible) so we could make improvements in the vice president's residence. We also got $200,000 from Congress after Marilyn invited staff director for the House Appropriations subcommittee Aubrey A. "Tex" Gunnels to visit the house. She asked him to intervene with Congress to get funds appropriated for renovations. The estimated Federal outlay for the VP's residence in 1991 was $626,000. The residence costs taxpayers $378,000 per year for care, maintenance and operations.

We added four new third floor bedrooms, a sitting room and office for Marilyn, new heating, cooling, wiring and plumbing, in addition to a swimming pool and a 30' by 30' putting green.

In 1991 I got a $46,545 pay raise, bringing my salary to $160,600. Ralph Nader urged taxpayers to protest, since the rest of the country was in a recession. I got a raise again on New Year's Day 1992: $5,600.

My assets have been estimated at around $1.4 million.

How much money do I really have?

*"I don't know. I suppose a critic could say
that that is a habit of people who have a lot
of money."*

In October 1990, Marilyn and our daughter, Corinne, took a
horseback ride in Manassas Battlefield National Park in Virginia.
Nothing unusual about that, except that the park was closed to
everyone else because President Bush had vetoed a Congressional
budget resolution and furloughed Federal workers.

A Manassas resident said this was the:

"epitome of arrogance."

The Park Service had approved construction of a six- to nine-stall
stable for my Secret Service horses that would have cost taxpayers an
estimated $50,000 to $75,000.

*"Without the connection to Quayle, these
stables probably wouldn't be built. They've
been shown to be unneeded and damaging to
the park's historic character,"*

said Bruce Craig, cultural resources program manager with the
National Parks and Conservation Association.

My press secretary, David Beckwith, said:

*"He's got a family. This is a great family
activity and he is just as pleased as he can
be."*

Rep. Ralph Regula (R-OH) said:

> *"The security of these children is very*
> *important. The vice president's children are*
> *as much entitled to live a life as anyone else."*

The House of Representatives voted for an amendment that would expressly forbid the Park Service from building the stables with government funds. On the bright side, though, a week earlier they decided not to cut my budget by the estimated $27,000 that my April 1991 golfing weekend in Augusta, Ga. cost the taxpayers.

Marilyn rides corporate jets when it's convenient, but she won't tell the press whose jets she uses and how often.

Meanwhile, I am "violently opposed" to a Democratic plan for an increase in the top tax rates paid by the wealthiest Americans.

> *"The so-called rich are paying a greater*
> *percentage of the taxes than in the past...*
> *Their definition of rich comes down to*
> *include darn near everybody."*

AP/Wide World Photo

"We're at a time now where there's so much baloney, any guy who's down to earth, who's organic and straightforward, is going to do well."

— Lee Atwater, former chairman of the Republican party

Ordinary People

In 1980 I rehearsed with a media consultant:

> *"I'm Dan Quayle. I'm Dan Quayle. I'm
> Dan Quayle. I am Dan Quayle. The real
> Dan Quayle. The real Dan Quayle stand up.
> I'm Dan Quayle. I'm Dan Quayle."*

In October 1988, I told a campaign rally:

> *"It's rural America. It's where I came from.
> We always refer to ourselves as real
> America. Rural America, real America,
> real, real America."*

I maintain that:

> *"You have to get out of Washington to find
> out what the real people are thinking,
> whether it's Lubbock [Texas], which is the
> new barometer to test what America really
> thinks, or Peoria or Muncie or Fort Wayne
> or wherever it may be."*

> *"I feel it in my gut, deep down in my gut.
> Trust old dad. It's my instinct. I don't care
> what your polls tell you. I'm listening to
> people on the street. You have to trust your
> instincts."*

Whenever I travel, I make stops to meet people. I get:

> *"a list of all the places along the route —*
> *restaurants, grocery stores and that sort of*
> *thing. Then [I] usually go over the list on the*
> *plane and decide where [I]want to stop."*

In a Hy-Vee grocery store in Cedar Rapids, Iowa, I bought a soft drink and said:

> *"I am convinced as the shoppers of Hy-Vee*
> *go, so goes the state of Iowa."*

My motorcade stopped at a Burger King in Ontario, California because I saw a "Help Wanted" sign in the window. I told the press:

> *"I want to show you an optimistic sign that*
> *things are beginning to turn around."*

Then I led them into the fast food restaurant where, sure enough, part-time jobs were available, paying $4.25/hour with no benefits:

> *"You have a part-time job, you have a job.*
> *That's better than no job at all."*

While visiting a Hardee's restaurant, I greeted a woman with a handshake and said:

> *"I'm Dan Quayle, who are you?"*

She replied:

> *"I'm your Secret Service agent."*

I'll never forget the time during the '88 campaign when we were at a garden center and produce store in Baltimore:

*"As we were walking around in the store,
Marilyn and I were just really impressed by
all of the novelties and the different types of
little things that you could get for Christmas.
And all the people that would help you, they
were dressed up in things that said 'I believe
in Santa Claus.' And the only thing that I
could think is that I believe in George Bush."*

I instructed my staff, which includes eight lawyers and seven Ph.D.s, to read *People* magazine to keep them in touch with the feelings of "real people" who live "in the real world."

In November 1990, I appeared on my favorite TV show, the CBS comedy "Major Dad," making a cameo appearance as myself in honor of the 215th anniversary of the Marine Corps.

I did a bit on the phone with Gunnery Sgt. Alva Bricker, the show's wacky female character, who swooned at the sound of my voice.

A reviewer said my performance as myself on "Major Dad" was:

"amazingly realistic."

Marj Hiner, one of the organizers of the Dan Quayle commemorative exhibition in Huntington, Ind., said of me:

*"What a role model for our children, to know
that you can be a normal person, come from
a normal family and become vice president of
the United States."*

Wilma Johnson, one of my admirers, with a cardboard cutout of me at the Dan Quayle Commemorative Exhibition, Huntington, Ind., 1990.

National Security meeting just after Iraq invaded Kuwait. Left to Right, Defense Secretary Dick Cheney, George Bush, me, then-White House Chief of Staff John Sununu, and CIA Director William Webster.

"I spend a great deal of time with the president. We have a very close, personal, loyal relationship. I'm not, as they say, a potted plant in these meetings."

— I said this in 1989

Back to the Future

"My full preoccupation right now is to be as good a vice president as I can.
I am interested in vice presidents who have served as presidents. I can't say the thought [of the presidency] hasn't crossed my mind."

"I try to stay away from liberalism. I know how dangerous it is for our...Don't ask me to take a liberal position where I am right now. It's contrary to the administration's viewpoints. It would not be terribly helpful to anyone, especially me."

"I'm making valuable contacts. We'll see what happens. Politics is interesting... I'm doing what is expected of me... Obviously, it gives me a lot flexibility down the road."

"I know what the president does on a day-to-day basis, how he goes about the job. I'm there. I'm present."

One of my senior advisers said,

"You can't pretend he's not interested in the presidency."

David Brinkley once called me "Mr. President" by mistake, and I gleefully exclaimed:

> *"Hey! Moving up!"*

I've assembled a team of advisers looking forward to 1996:

> *"We will lay the groundwork for our next great triumph; a fifth straight conservative victory in the year 1996."*

Here I am in the Oval Office.

Appendix: Awards

1) **Honorary Doctor of Laws**

   1982, DePauw University

   Faculty secretly voted 32-24 against awarding the degree.

2) **John and Sally McNaughton Memorial Award**

   October 26, 1990, DePauw University

   For distinguished public service.

3) **Skipper's Little Buddy Award**

   November 1990, Gilligan's Island Fan Club

   I refused this award on "ethical" grounds.

4) **Inducted into the Little League Hall of Excellence**

   December 6, 1990, Little League Hall of Excellence

   Criteria for induction:
   1) Must have played Little League ball;
   2) Must have achieved a position of responsibility;
   3) Must be a role model for children.

Other inductees: Senator Bill Bradley; former major league pitcher Tom Seaver.

5) **Most deserving of medals for bravery at a great distance from battle.**

April, 1991, **The Nonviolent Activist**

Along with Stephen Solarz and Alphonse D'Amato:

> *"The three men share in common a total enthusiasm for someone else fighting their battles. Some say hawks, we say chicken hawks."*

6) **IgNobel Prize for Education**

October 3, 1991, MIT and **The** Journal of Irreproducible Results

For being "a consumer of time and occupier of space, for demonstrating, better than anyone else, the need for science education."

7) **Patriot Award**

October 16, 1991, Congressional Medal of Honor Society

For being, in the words of the president of the society, a "true American."

Country singer Lee Greenwood, who wrote the song "God Bless the U.S.A.," also received a Patriot Award.

Richard McCool, 69, who was awarded the Congressional Medal of Honor after a kamikaze plane smashed into his ship in 1945, resigned from the Society upon learning of the Quayle award, saying:

> *"For an organization that is composed of people who have all served in the Armed forces — and served very well — to give this award to someone who did everything he could to avoid military service is inappropriate."*

8) Asshole of the Month

September 1991, Hustler *magazine*

For his visit to the Persian Gulf.

9) Golden Bull Award

December 1991, Plain English Campaign

For his statement:

"It is necessary to restate the President's viewpoint very clearly, and that is that we are a party that is diversified. We are a party that, though we have a position on abortion, that those who disagree with us should not feel excluded because of that issue. We do, in former Chairman Lee Atwater's words, offer the party as a big tent, and therefore that message has to be clear. How we do that within the platform, the preamble to the platform or whatnot, remains to be seen, but the message will have to be articulated with great clarity."

Bibliography

Becker, Jim and Andy Meyer and Bron Smith. *Where's Dan Quayle?* Collier Books, 1991.

Black, Christine M. and Thomas Oliphant. *All By Myself: The Unmaking of a Presidential Campaign*, Globe Pequot Press, 1989.

Blumenthal, Sidney. *Pledging Allegiance: The Last Campaign of the Cold War*, Harper Collins, 1990.

Fenno, Richard. *The Making of a Senator: Dan Quayle*, Congressional Quarterly Press, 1989.

Ide, Arthur Frederick. *Quayle Droppings*, Liberal Press, 1988.

Ide, Arthur Frederick. *Bush-Quayle, the Reagan Legacy*, Scholars Books, 1989.

Newsweek. The Quest for the Presidency 1988, Touchstone, 1989.

Quayle, Marilyn, and Nancy Honeycutt. *Embrace the Serpent*, Crown, 1992.

Slansky, Paul. *The Clothes Have No Emperor: A Chronicle of the American 80s*, Simon and Schuster Fireside, 1989.

Solomon, Jeremy and Ken Brady. *The Dan Quayle Quiz Book*, Little, Brown, 1989.

Twentieth Century Fund. *A Heartbeat Away*. Priority Press, 1988.

Wills, Garry. *Under God: Religion and American Politics*, Simon and Schuster, 1990.

Witcover, Jules and Jack Germond. *Whose Broad Stripes and Bright Stars: The Trivial Pursuit of the Presidency 1988*, Warner Books, 1989.

Witcover, Jules. *Crapshoot: Rolling the Dice on the Vice Presidency*, Crown, 1992.

Notes

Acknowledgements
"People that are really very weird..." *The New Republic*, 10/31/88

Foreword
"Inexperience in the Oval Office..." *The New Yorker*, 10/10/88
"Man of the future..." *The Indianapolis Star*, 8/17/88
"Votes from women..." *The Kansas City* (Missouri)*Times*, 8/18/88
"Man of character..." *The Indianapolis Star*, 8/20/88
"One of Indiana's finest..." *The Kansas City* (Missouri)*Times*, 8/18/88
"Bum rap in the press..." *The New York Times*, 5/9/91
"Take out the word 'Quayle'..." *The Baltimore Sun*, 1/17/92
"My choice..." *The Indianapolis Star*, 8/17/88
"I'm 64 and he's 41..." *Kansas City* (Missouri) *Times*, 8/18/88
    (Note: Bush is now 68 and Quayle is 45.)
"He did not go to Canada..." Slansky, p. 250

Preface
"What a waste..." NAACP luncheon, Nashville, Tenn., 5/15/89

Timeline
Birth announcement... *The Indiana Reporter*, 2/5/1947
Teen-Age Republicans... *The Quayle Quarterly*, Spring/90
"Not a good student..." *The Boston Globe*, 8/20/88
"Should have pursued..." *The New York Times*, 6/25/89
"Far greater sacrifice in Vietnam..." *The Washington Post*, 7/14/90
"Just a job..." Blumenthal, pp. 276-277
"I treat her as staff person..." *The Washington Post*, 10/20/88
"70% of the world's lawyers..." *The Chicago Tribune*, 8/13/91
"Never had to work really hard..." *The Los Angeles Times*, 8/17/88

"To elect the representatives..." *The Los Angeles Times*, 11/2/88
"I'm a Republican..." *Lake County Senate Debate, Indiana*, 10/17/80
"You can get a bunch of guys..." Fenno, p. 18
"Whole career in public service..." *AP*, 10/9/91
"With me, the future..." *The New Republic*, 10/31/88
"Batman fan..." *The Chicago Tribune*, 10/25/89

Roots

"Family is something which goes..." *Los Angeles Times*, 11/7/88
"You can do anything..." Vice pres. debate, Omaha, Neb., 10/5/88
"Happy have we met..." Fenno, p. 126
Later in life, Grandpa... *The Boston Globe*, 8/21/88
When I was chosen for vice pres. ... *The Indianapolis Star*, 8/17/88
"Little League baseball is..." *The New York Times*, 11/25/90
"I love California..." *The San Francisco Chronicle*, 2/9/91
"Republicans understand..." *In These Times*, 9/27/88
"Playing golf..." *The New York Times*, 10/31/88
Poem about my father... *The New York Times*, 5/14/91
It "was like meeting..." *The Washington Post*, 10/2/88
Our dinner table conversation...*The New Republic*, 10/31/88

Ferris Bueller's Day Off

"I was in college with the guy..." *The Boston Globe*, 8/20/88
We "went to the drive-in..." Ann Schacht Pfister, *Fame*, 2/89
Head of the Teen-Age Republicans... *Fame*, 2/89
"He didn't know Goldwater's platform..." *Fame*, 2/89
"Dan was so determined..." *Fame*, 2/89
"I didn't pay a lot of attention..." *The Wall Street Journal*, 11/15/91
My Dad described my college years... *Fame*, 2/89
"Girls, golf and alcohol"...*The Boston Globe*, 8/21/88
"This is in 1968..." *The Boston Globe*, 8/21/88
Failed senior comprehensive exam... *The Washington Post*, 10/2/88

2.16 GPA... *The Washington Post*, 1/7/92
"A less than serious student..." *U.S. News and World Report*, 9/12/88

All Quiet on the Midwestern Front
"We kept thinking..." *The Indianapolis Star*, 8/20/88
"You call home..." *The Washington Post*, 1/7/92
"I hoped he would help me..." *The New Orleans Times- Picayune*, 8/20/88
"Got into the Guard fairly..." *The Indianapolis Star*, 8/20/88
"We never failed to have a good time..." *The Indianapolis Star*, 8/19/88
"I wouldn't call us slackers..." *The Indianapolis Star*, 8/19/88
"He partied like the rest of us..." *The Indianapolis Star*, 8/19/88
"My problem with the war..." *The New Orleans Times-Picayune*, 8/20/88
"those men and women who sacrificed..." *The Kansas City Times*, 8/18/88

High Times
"I don't care if Danny smoked pot..." *The Indianapolis News*, 11/8/91
"Wedding present..." *High Times*, 2/89
"We should concentrate on..." *The Fort Wayne Sentinel*, 3/16/77
DEA investigation... *The New York Times*, 11/7/91
"Not just a youthful indiscretion..." *The Village Voice*, 12/27/88
"You are losing your children..." *The Los Angeles Times*, 8/9/90
Veep in charge of the war on drugs... *The New York Times*, 5/27/88
"I haven't read 'Doonesbury'..." *USA Today*, 11/14/91
"The American public as a whole is smoking less..." *The Wall Street Journal*, 9/27/90
"Tobacco industry should continue to expand..." *The San Diego Daily Transcript*, 7/19/90

The Paper Chase

"Somehow he got in..." *The Boston Globe*, 8/21/88
"It enabled me to go to law school..." *The New Orleans Times-Picayune*, 8/20/88
My grades... *The Washington Post*, 1/7/92
Admitted to law school... *The Cleveland Plain Dealer*, 9/9/88
"The program was not aimed to benefit wealthy..." *The Cleveland Plain Dealer*, 9/9/88
"No rules were broken..." *Cleveland Plain Dealer*, 9/10/88
"I deserve respect..." *Manhattan Inc.*, 11/88
2.71 GPA, *The Washington Post*, 1/7/92

She Stoops to Conquer

"He was an equal to me..." *The Washington Post*, 10/20/88
Ode to the Flipster... Birthday poem written by Marilyn's friends, *USA Weekend*, 11/3/91
My "intellectual curiosity..." *The Boston Globe*, 9/22/88
"We thought it was a joke..." *New York Newsday*, 10/24/88
"My role as an adviser to him... *The Washington Post*, 10/20/88
"The only thing Marilyn wouldn't..." *New York Newsday*, 10/24/88
My guest appearance on "Major Dad"... *The Quayle Quarterly*, Spring/Summer/91
"It hurt..." *The Indianapolis News*, 6/6/90
"I'm having fun..." The Los Angeles Times, 11/27/89
Marilyn in Bangladesh... *The Fort Wayne Journal-Gazette*, 5/23/91
this outspokenness might offend... *Newsweek*, 7/2/90
her new novel... *Publishers Weekly*, 2/3/92
my staff learns what Marilyn is up to... *The Los Angeles Times*, 11/27/89
"When I look at my life..." *Brockton* (Massachusetts) *Enterprise*, 10/28/90
"We both overmarried..." *Newsweek*, 11/19/90

Everything You've Always Wanted to Know About Sex
"He would rather play golf than have sex..." *New York Newsday*,
10/24/88
"Sex-for-votes" scandal... *The Congressional Quarterly*, 3/21/81
She turned me down... *Penthouse*, 11/88
Wooden doll... *The Washington Post*, 3/12/90
"To emphasize abstinence..." *The Woodland Hills* (California)*Daily
News*, 11/9/91

Heaven Can Wait
"Never surrender to what is right..." *The Quayle Quarterly*,
Winter/Spring/92
"Religion is everything to me..." *Men's Life*, 10/90
"I read Dr. Thieme's literature..." *The Louisville* (Kentucky)
Courier-Journal, 10/88
"She doesn't listen to them now..." *The New York Daily News*,
10/10/88
"I really don't associate myself..." Fenno, p. 9
"As one Christian to another..." Fenno, p. 17

Caddyshack
"I wanted to be a golf pro..." *Spy*, 12/91
My golf bag once saved... *Birmingham* (Alabama) *News*, 2/22/90
The "football"... *The Indianapolis Star*, 6/14/90
My handicap... *The Detroit Free Press*, 3/11/90
"Scorecard"... *The Indianapolis Star*, 9/2/90
$27,000 golf trip... AP, 5/1/91
Play at restricted clubs... *New York Newsday*, 12/31/90
"Not going to protest Burning Tree..." AP, 12/28/90
"He goes on a high..." *The Washington Post*, 1/8/92
"Can't get enough..." *The Washington Post*, 1/8/92

The Candidate

"I'll have to check with my dad..." *The Washington Post*, 10/2/88

"Go ahead; you won't win..." *The Washington Post*, 10/2/88

"Danny's dream..." *The Washington Post*, 10/2/88.

Note: Pope later said the movie "The Man", starring James Earl Jones, inspired Quayle to seek public office (Witcover, p. 368).

"I never thought about running for Congress..." Fenno, p. 3

"I wouldn't consider it unless..." Fenno, p. 4

I sent Redford an autographed picture of myself... *The New Orleans Times-Picayune*, 8/17/88

In the 1980 Senate campaign... *Indianapolis Star*, 8/17/88

"Hello everybody, I'm Dan Quayle..." Slansky, p.258

"That's what it takes to win!..." *Vogue*, 2/91

"I beat incumbents..." *The Wall Street Journal*, 10/11/90

"The boy's retarded..." *West*, 4/14/91

Go to the dentist... *The Washington Post*, 11/9/88

"I'm not impressed..." *Auburn Evening Star*, 2/15/77

"My first year..." Fenno, p. 30

"This is my first year..." Fenno, p. 30

"The only thing Congress is interested in..." "Nightline", 11/4/91

Bush campaigned for me... *The Indianapolis Star*, 9/10/78

"What are we going to say about me..." Fenno, pp. 4-5

"If I had not run for the Senate..." Fenno, p. 18

"His attendance record was lousy..." Fenno, p. 12

I missed meetings... *The Washingtonian*, 10/80

Missed homeless veterans' bill vote... *The Boston Globe*, 8/26/88

"One committee I don't want..." Fenno, p. 20

"About a quarter of an inch deep..." *The Washington Post*, 1/11/81

Cut off food stamps... Witcover, p. 370

Tax credit for people who lose weight or stop smoking... *The Gary* (Indiana) *Post-Tribune*, 7/12/90

Tax break for golf pros... *The New York Times*, 7/18/86

Job Training Partnership Act... Fenno, p. 150

"Hearings on it around the state..." Fenno, p. 151
JTPA "an awful mess..." *The Quayle Quarterly*, Summer/90
"A welfare system..." *The Quayle Quarterly*, Summer/90
"Twelve most underrated..." *Politics in America*, 9/85
"There are no failures..." Fenno, p. 162
"I'm still flying high..." Fenno, p. 167
"Term limits..." *The Wall Street Journal*, 9/28/90

Fear and Loathing on the Campaign Trail '88
"I stand by all the misstatements..." "Prime Time Live," 8/17/89
"One word sums up..." "Larry King Live," 12/6/89
"A vice president very much like George Bush was..." *New York*, 3/13/89
"Well, now, what..." *The Washington Post*, 1/7/92
"Let's go get 'em..." *The Washington Post*, 1/7/92
"Why did you let him?..." Witcover and Germond, p. 436
Vice presidential debate, Omaha, Neb., 10/5/88
"Baptism of fire..." UPI, 6/5/90
"Was my confidence shaken?..." *The Wall Street Journal*, 11/15/91

It's a Mad, Mad, Mad, Mad World
"Irreversible trend..." *The Wall Street Journal*, 5/26/89
"You can meet a lot of people..." *The Progressive*, 3/89
"Happy campers..." *Newsweek*, 5/8/89
"Elimination of human rights in El Salvador..." *In These Times*, 3/1/89
"Who would have predicted that Dubcek..." "Larry King Live," 12/6/89
"I felt like I was in charge..." *Telegram & Gazette*, 2/1/90
I phoned Richard Nixon... *The New York Daily News*, 6/20/89
"The people that I met..." "Good Morning America," 1/30/90
"Smile discreetly..." *The Gary* (Indiana) *Post-Tribune*, 3/16/90

Richard Nixon concerned about image... *The San Francisco Chronicle*, 9/26/91
"The political instincts I have..." *The New York Times*, 4/30/89

How to Succeed in Business
"A nefarious, secret kind of government..." UPI, 7/7/91
"The president gave me this task... *The Wall Street Journal*, 7/11/90
"When it's wet, it's wet..." *New York Newsday*, 9/9/91
"Our future competitiveness..." UPI, 6/6/90
"If someone has deep pockets, just let them pay..." *The Wall Street Journal*, 7/11/90
"Beyond public accountability..." *The Baltimore Sun*, 11/18/91
"I do have a political agenda..." *Business Week*, 11/4/91

The Last Frontier
"Mars is essentially in the same orbit..." CNN, 11/18/89
"Can NASA do the job..." *The Quayle Quarterly*, Winter/Spring/91
"I didn't understand..." *The New Republic*, 5/15/89
"The importance of the space station..." *The Quayle Quarterly*, Summer/Fall/91
Tom Clancy... *Newsweek*, 6/5/89
"The real thing..." *Newsweek*, 9/5/88
"Space program should always go full throttle up..." AP, 2/20/91
"We are leaders of the world..." *The New York Times*, 1/13/92
"Children take space trip..." *The Los Angeles Times*, 5/6/91

Blackboard Jungle
IgNobel Prize for Education... *The Boston Globe*, 10/3/91
"Teachers are the only profession..." *The New Republic*, 11/26/90
"We will move..." *The New York Times*, 6/25/89
"The best educated American people in the world..." *The Los Angeles Times*, 10/2/88

The Red Badge of Courage
"We are ready..." *The Columbus* (Ohio) *Dispatch*, 9/27/90
"The world is still a dangerous place..." UPI, 5/28/90
"He's been in every meeting..." *The Fort Wayne* (Indiana) *Journal-Gazette*, 1/20/91
"Before he left for vacation..." *The San Francisco Examiner*, 8/90
"Vietnam is a jungle..." *The Wall Street Journal*, 1/11/91
"Truly a just war..." *The Los Angeles Times*, 2/8/91
Disclosed Stealth base... *The London Observer*, 2/3/91
"$600 toilet seats..." *The Los Angeles Times*, 2/9/91
"The making of mistakes..." *The Boston Globe*, 9/28/88
"Nuclear weapons an option..." *The Los Angeles Times*, 2/2/91
"Partisanship above statesmanship..." *The New York Times*, 12/12/90
"Anti-war demonstrations..." *The New York Post*, 1/24/91
"A stirring victory..." *The Fresno* (California) *Bee*, 4/13/91

Other People's Money
"If we don't succeed..." *The Phoenix Gazette*, 3/28/90
"I'm cashing in..." *The Washington Times*, 7/24/90
I raised about $16 million... AP, 10/29/90
"Very effective fund-raising tool..." AP, 7/24/90
People paid... AP, 7/24/90
I appeared... *The Indianapolis Star*, 9/5/90
You could have dined... *The New York Daily News*, 6/17/90
$20,000 to play a round of golf... *Golf Digest*, 5/90
"One thing we're able to do..." *The Detroit Free Press*, 9/15/90
"Money wins..." *Vogue*, 2/90

The Ruling Classes
"You don't make money in politics..." *The Detroit News*, 9/15/90
Adjusted gross income... *The Indianapolis Star*, 4/17/91
Marilyn invited "Tex" Gunnels... *The Gary* (Indiana) *Post-Tribune*, 12/2/90

Federal outlay for the VP's residence... *The Washington Post Magazine*, 3/10/91

Swimming pool and putting green... *Gary,* Indiana, *Post-Tribune,* 12/2/90

My assets... *The Indianapolis Star*, 5/16/91

"A habit of people who have a lot of money..." *The Washington Post*, 1/7/92

The "epitome of arrogance..." *The Quayle Quarterly*, Spring/Summer/91

Stable for Secret Service horses... *The Potomac News*, 9/22/90

"Without the connection to Quayle..." *National Parks*, 4/91

"This is a great family activity..." *The Quayle Quarterly*, Spring/Summer 1991

"The security of these children..." AP, 6/25/91

The House of Representatives voted against... *The Fort Wayne* (Indiana) *Journal Gazette*, 6/19/91; AP, 6/25/91

Marilyn rides corporate jets... *The New York Daily News*, 6/19/91

I am "violently opposed"... AP, 10/12/90

"The so-called rich..." *The Washington Post*, 11/11/90

Ordinary People

"We're at a time now where there's so much baloney..." *The Washington Post*, 4/2/91

"I'm Dan Quayle..." Blumenthal, p. 275

"It's rural America..." *The Wall Street Journal*, 10/21/88

"You have to get out of Washington..." *The Fort Wayne* (Indiana) *Journal-Gazette*, 3/9/89

"I feel it in my gut..." Fenno, p. 163

"A list of all the places along the route..." *The Los Angeles Times*, 7/9/90

"As the shoppers of Hy-Vee go..." *The Minnesota Daily*, 10/90

Burger King help wanted... AP, 1/21/92

"I'm Dan Quayle, who are you?..." *Newsweek*, 2/26/90

106

"I believe in George Bush..." *The Los Angeles Times*, 11/16/88
I instructed my staff to read *People*... *U.S. News & World Report*, 4/29/91
I appeared on "Major Dad"... *The Washington Times*, 11/5/90
"Amazingly realistic..." *The Dover-New Philadelphia*, Ohio, *Times Reporter*, 10/18/90
"What a role model for our children..." *The New York Times*, 5/14/91

Back to the Future
"I spend a great deal of time ..." *New York Newsday*, 12/31/89
"My full preoccupation..." *The San Francisco Examiner*, 6/23/91
"Stay away from liberalism..." *The San Francisco Examiner*, 6/23/91
"I'm making valuable contacts..." *The Chicago Tribune*, 10/19/90
"I know what the president does..." *New York Newsday*, 12/31/89
"You can't pretend he's not interested in the presidency..." *The Orange County Register*, 1/4/90
"Hey! Moving up!" Meet the Press, 2/23/92
"We will lay the groundwork..." *The New York Times*, 2/22/92

Appendix A: Awards
Honorary Doctor of Laws... *The Boston Globe*, 8/20/88
John and Sally McNaughton Memorial Award... *The Indianapolis News*, 10/26/90
Skipper's Little Buddy... *The Miami Herald*, 11/3/90
Little League Hall of Excellence... Associated Press, 11/20/90
Most deserving... *The Nonviolent Activist*, 4/91
IgNobel Prize for Education... *The Boston Globe*, 10/3/91
Patriot Award... *The Oregonian*, 10/16/1991
Richard McCool resigns... *The Seattle Post-Intelligencer*, 10/31/91
Asshole of the Month... *Hustler*, 9/91
Golden Bull Award... *The New York Times*, 12/4/91

The Quayle Quarterly™

Volume 2 - Number 3   *A Watchful Eye on the Vice Presidency*™   Summer/Fall 1991 $3.95

Faint of Heart

by Jefferson Morley

George Bush's atrial fibrillation "sent a nervous electrical charge through the collective cardiovascular system," noted columnist Ellen Goodman. Who didn't feel that national psychological jolt while unfolding the newspaper on that May morning? It rippled from front porches to newsstands to barroom TVs. From Takoma Park, Maryland to Bridgeport, Connecticut to Compton, California to Minneapolis, Minnesota, the psychological reaction was the same stunned disbelief: "President Quayle?"

Robert Beckel, a political pundit on CNN's "Crossfire" show, predicted that the stock market would drop 600 points on the day that Dan Quayle became president. Johnny Carson said, "Dan Quayle is getting nervous." Pause. "He's been studying the Cliff Notes to the Constitution." The pollsters went out and confirmed what the comedians knew long ago: the country doesn't take Dan Quayle seriously. Only 19 percent of people polled said they would consider voting for Quayle for president. The Vice President tried to play it off. "If 81 percent go for Bush, and 19 percent go for me," quipped Quayle, "then we've got just about everybody." Gong.

The much-abused Veep was, however, soon getting the best press of his life. For all of the complaints about the "liberal" media's coverage of Quayle, one of the strongest pockets of pro-Quayle sentiment in the country is found in the Washington press corps. The pro-Quayle faction expressed itself primarily in three publications often described as "liberal": *The New York Times*, *The Washington Post*, and *The New Republic*. Quayle's champions were A.M. Rosenthal and William Safire of *The New York*

(continued on page 16)

Next in Line

Inside this Issue

Nuclear Reactionary

by Ralph Nader and Bill Magavern

Last year, the Nuclear Regulatory Commission (NRC) approved a policy to deregulate many radioactive substances and allow nuclear wastes to be buried in landfills, burned in incinerators, or recycled into consumer products. The commissioners, who are more lapdogs than watchdogs of the nuclear industry, specifically suggested frying pans and jewelry as consumer products that could incorporate radiation. The NRC has also said that contaminated nuclear sites could be left with some residual radioactivity and used as "children's playgrounds" or "child care centers."

A Maryland resident, justifiably outraged by the NRC's dangerous "Below Regulatory Concern" policy, called the Vice President. Twenty minutes later, Dan Quayle called her back. The citizen explained that the Federal government was trying to increase the amount of cancer-causing radiation in the environment. Quayle replied, "You know, the NRC is there to protect you." When she disagreed, the Veep hung up on her.

Quayle's laissez-faire attitude toward nuclear regulation is embodied in the Administration's National Energy Strategy (NES), which envisions building more than 100 new nuclear plants. In order to jump-start the moribund nuclear power industry—no new plants have been ordered since 1978—the NES proposes to run roughshod over the democratic rights of citizens and their state and local governments. The Bush-Quayle Department of Energy and their friends in the nuclear lobby would have us believe that their inability to build any more plants is due not to radioactive waste, cost overruns, dangerous technology and mismanaged facilities, but to an excess of democracy.

The NES proposes to amend the Atomic Energy Act to take away citizens' rights

(continued on page 18)